YORK NOTES

MACBETH

AQA PRACTICE TESTS
WITH ANSWERS

ALISON POWELL

The right of Alison Powell to be identified as the Author of this Work
has been asserted by her in accordance with the Copyright,
Designs and Patents Act 1988

YORK PRESS
322 Old Brompton Road, London SW5 9JH

PEARSON EDUCATION LIMITED
Edinburgh Gate, Harlow,
Essex CM20 2JE, United Kingdom
Associated companies, branches and representatives throughout the world

First published 2018

10 9 8 7 6 5 4 3 2 1

ISBN 978–1–2922–3682–7

Phototypeset by Swales and Willis Ltd

Photo credits: Rawpixel/© iStock for page 6 bottom / Syda Productions/
Shutterstock for page 50 bottom

CONTENTS

PART ONE: INTRODUCTION

How to use these practice tests

This book contains seven GCSE English Literature exam-style practice tests for *Macbeth*. All the York Notes tests have been modelled on the ones that you will sit in your AQA GCSE 9–1 English Literature exam.

There are lots of ways these tests can support your study and revision for your AQA English Literature exam on *Macbeth*. There is no 'right' way – choose the one (or ones) that suits your learning style best.

1 Alongside the York Notes Study Guide for *Macbeth*

Do you have the York Notes Study Guide for *Macbeth*?

These tests will allow you to try out all the skills and techniques outlined in the Study Guide. So you could:

- choose a question from this book
- read the sections of the Study Guide relevant to the question, i.e. Plot and Action; Characters; Themes, Contexts and Setting; Structure, Form and Language
- use the Progress Booster exam section of the Study Guide to remind yourself of key exam techniques
- complete the question.

2 As a stand-alone revision programme

Do you know the text inside out and have you already mastered the skills needed for your exam?

If so, you can keep your skills fresh by answering one or two questions from this book each day or week in the lead-up to the exam. You could make a revision diary and allocate particular questions to particular times.

3 As a form of mock exam

Would you like to test yourself under exam conditions?

You could put aside part of a day to work on a practice test in a quiet room. Set a stopwatch so that you can experience what it will be like in your real exam. If some of your friends have copies of this book then several of you could all do this together and discuss your answers afterwards.

Or, you could try working through Part Two of this book slowly, question by question, over a number of days as part of your revision, and save the further questions in Part Three to use as a mock test nearer the exam.

How to use the answer sections

This book contains a mixture of annotated sample answers and short (indicative content) answers that will help you to:

- identify the difference between Mid, Good and Very High Level work
- understand how the Assessment Objectives are applied
- grade your own answers by comparing them with the samples provided.

The answers can also give you additional ideas for your responses and help you to aim high.

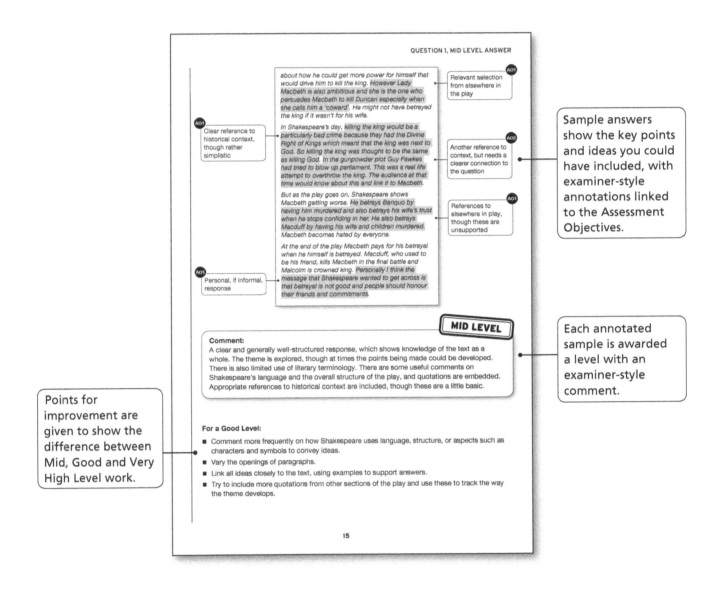

QUESTION 1, MID LEVEL ANSWER

about how he could get more power for himself that would drive him to kill the king. However Lady Macbeth is also ambitious and she is the one who persuades Macbeth to kill Duncan especially when she calls him a 'coward'. He might not have betrayed the king if it wasn't for his wife.

AO1 Relevant selection from elsewhere in the play

AO1 Clear reference to historical context, though rather simplistic

In Shakespeare's day, killing the king would be a particularly bad crime because they had the Divine Right of Kings which meant that the king was next to God. So killing the king was thought to be the same as killing God. In the gunpowder plot Guy Fawkes had tried to blow up parliament. This was a real life attempt to overthrow the king. The audience at that time would know about this and link it to Macbeth.

AO3 Another reference to context, but needs a clearer connection to the question

But as the play goes on, Shakespeare shows Macbeth getting worse. He betrays Banquo by having him murdered and also betrays his wife's trust when he stops confiding in her. He also betrays Macduff by having his wife and children murdered. Macbeth becomes hated by everyone.

AO1 References to elsewhere in play, though these are unsupported

At the end of the play Macbeth pays for his betrayal when he himself is betrayed. Macduff, who used to be his friend, kills Macbeth in the final battle and Malcolm is crowned king. Personally I think the message that Shakespeare wanted to get across is that betrayal is not good and people should honour their friends and commitments.

AO1 Personal, if informal, response

MID LEVEL

Comment:
A clear and generally well-structured response, which shows knowledge of the text as a whole. The theme is explored, though at times the points being made could be developed. There is also limited use of literary terminology. There are some useful comments on Shakespeare's language and the overall structure of the play, and quotations are embedded. Appropriate references to historical context are included, though these are a little basic.

For a Good Level:
- Comment more frequently on how Shakespeare uses language, structure, or aspects such as characters and symbols to convey ideas.
- Vary the openings of paragraphs.
- Link all ideas closely to the text, using examples to support answers.
- Try to include more quotations from other sections of the play and use these to track the way the theme develops.

15

Sample answers show the key points and ideas you could have included, with examiner-style annotations linked to the Assessment Objectives.

Each annotated sample is awarded a level with an examiner-style comment.

Points for improvement are given to show the difference between Mid, Good and Very High Level work.

Assessment Objectives and weightings

Your work on *Macbeth* will be examined through the four Assessment Objectives (AOs) listed below:

AO1	Read, understand and respond to texts. You should be able to: ● maintain a critical style and develop an informed personal response ● use textual references, including quotations, to support and illustrate interpretations.
AO2	Analyse the language, form and structure used by a writer to create meanings and effects, using relevant subject terminology where appropriate.
AO3	Show understanding of the relationships between texts and the contexts in which they were written.
AO4	Use a range of vocabulary and sentence structures, for clarity, purpose and effect, with accurate spelling and punctuation.

The marks allocated by AQA for each Assessment Objective are as follows:

AO1	12 marks
AO2	12 marks
AO3	6 marks
Total (per question)	**30 marks***

* Plus an additional 4 marks for AO4.

Knowing the number of marks allowed for each AO is important, as this will help you to achieve the right balance of key skills and techniques in your answer.

Mark scheme

The annotated sample answers that follow Questions 1 to 4 in this book have been given a Level based on the mark schemes below.*

Lower Level

AO1	You give some relevant responses to the set task and use some suitable references.
AO2	You identify some of the writer's methods but do not always comment effectively on them.
AO3	You show some awareness of contextual factors but find it difficult to link them to the text.
AO4	Your use of spelling, grammar and punctuation is rather inconsistent but does not usually impede meaning. Sentences and vocabulary are straightforward, with little variation.

Mid Level

AO1	You give a clear response and select suitable references and quotations.
AO2	You make clear references to the writer's methods to support your points.
AO3	You make clear links between some aspects of context and the text.
AO4	You spell and punctuate with general accuracy and use a range of vocabulary and sentences.

Turn to page 8 for the mark schemes for Good to High and Very High Levels.

These are 'student-friendly' mark schemes and are a guide only.

Good to High Level

AO1	You demonstrate very effective understanding of the task and text, and choose references and quotations carefully.
AO2	You analyse carefully and comment consistently well on the writer's methods, interpreting ideas.
AO3	You make very effective links between context and the text.
AO4	Your spelling, punctuation and grammar is very consistent and shows generally excellent control of meaning.

Very High Level

AO1	You have a broad, conceptualised idea of the text, and make well-judged and wide-ranging use of references and quotations.
AO2	You are analytical and explore the text precisely and convincingly. You comment in finely tuned detail on the writer's use of language, form and structure.
AO3	You write convincingly and relevantly about a wide range of contextual factors.
AO4	Your spelling, punctuation and grammar is very accurate and shows excellent control of meaning.

Now you know what you're aiming for, you can begin the practice tests.

Turn to page 10 for Question 1.

PART TWO: YORK NOTES PRACTICE TESTS WITH ANNOTATED SAMPLE ANSWERS

Question 1

Read the following extract from Act I Scene 7 of *Macbeth* and then answer the question that follows.

At this point in the play, Macbeth is speaking. He is questioning his own reasons for wanting to murder King Duncan.

> **MACBETH**
>
>   He's here in double trust:
> First, as I am his kinsman and his subject,
> Strong both against the deed; then, as his host,
> Who should against his murderer shut the door,
> 5   Not bear the knife myself. Besides, this Duncan
> Hath borne his faculties so meek, hath been
> So clear in his great office, that his virtues
> Will plead like angels, trumpet-tongued, against
> The deep damnation of his taking-off;
> 10 And Pity, like a naked new-born babe
> Striding the blast, or heaven's cherubim, horsed
> Upon the sightless curriers of the air,
> Shall blow the horrid deed in every eye,
> That tears shall drown the wind. I have no spur
> 15 To prick the sides of my intent but only
> Vaulting ambition, which o'erleaps itself
> And falls on the other.

Starting with this speech, explore how Shakespeare presents the theme of betrayal.

Write about:

- how Shakespeare presents the theme of betrayal in this speech
- how Shakespeare presents the theme of betrayal in the play as a whole.

[30 marks]
AO4 [4 marks]

Annotated sample answers

Now, read the three sample answers that follow and, based on what you have read, try to allocate a level to your own work. Which of the three responses is your answer closest to? Don't be discouraged if your work doesn't seem as strong as some of the responses here – the point is to use these samples to learn about what is needed and then put it into practice in your own work. Conversely, you may have mentioned relevant ideas or points that don't appear in these responses; if this is the case, give yourself a pat on the back – it shows you are considering lots of good ideas.

Sample answer A

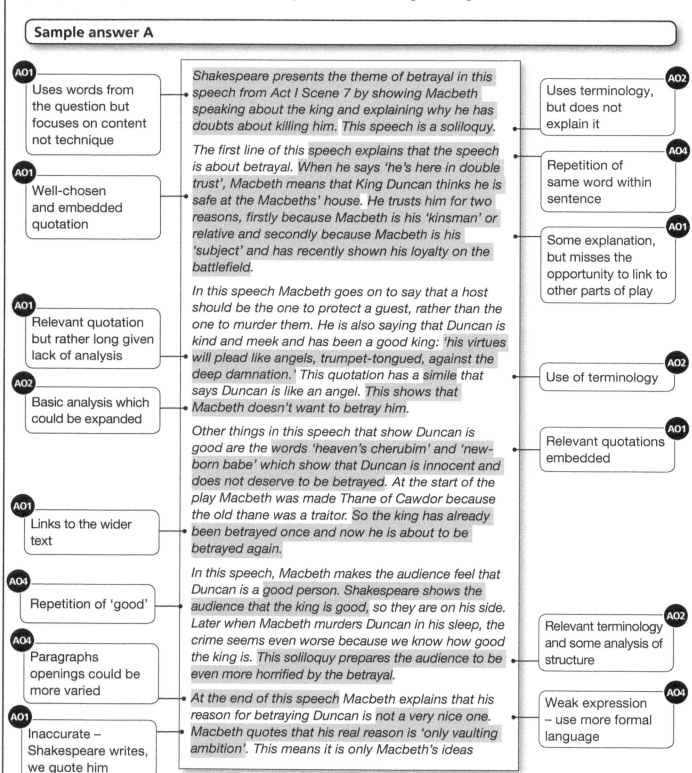

AO1 Uses words from the question but focuses on content not technique

AO1 Well-chosen and embedded quotation

AO1 Relevant quotation but rather long given lack of analysis

AO2 Basic analysis which could be expanded

AO1 Links to the wider text

AO4 Repetition of 'good'

AO4 Paragraphs openings could be more varied

AO1 Inaccurate – Shakespeare writes, we quote him

Shakespeare presents the theme of betrayal in this speech from Act I Scene 7 by showing Macbeth speaking about the king and explaining why he has doubts about killing him. This speech is a soliloquy.

The first line of this speech explains that the speech is about betrayal. When he says 'he's here in double trust', Macbeth means that King Duncan thinks he is safe at the Macbeths' house. He trusts him for two reasons, firstly because Macbeth is his 'kinsman' or relative and secondly because Macbeth is his 'subject' and has recently shown his loyalty on the battlefield.

In this speech Macbeth goes on to say that a host should be the one to protect a guest, rather than the one to murder them. He is also saying that Duncan is kind and meek and has been a good king: 'his virtues will plead like angels, trumpet-tongued, against the deep damnation.' This quotation has a simile that says Duncan is like an angel. This shows that Macbeth doesn't want to betray him.

Other things in this speech that show Duncan is good are the words 'heaven's cherubim' and 'new-born babe' which show that Duncan is innocent and does not deserve to be betrayed. At the start of the play Macbeth was made Thane of Cawdor because the old thane was a traitor. So the king has already been betrayed once and now he is about to be betrayed again.

In this speech, Macbeth makes the audience feel that Duncan is a good person. Shakespeare shows the audience that the king is good, so they are on his side. Later when Macbeth murders Duncan in his sleep, the crime seems even worse because we know how good the king is. This soliloquy prepares the audience to be even more horrified by the betrayal.

At the end of this speech Macbeth explains that his reason for betraying Duncan is not a very nice one. Macbeth quotes that his real reason is 'only vaulting ambition'. This means it is only Macbeth's ideas

AO2 Uses terminology, but does not explain it

AO4 Repetition of same word within sentence

AO1 Some explanation, but misses the opportunity to link to other parts of play

AO2 Use of terminology

AO1 Relevant quotations embedded

AO2 Relevant terminology and some analysis of structure

AO4 Weak expression – use more formal language

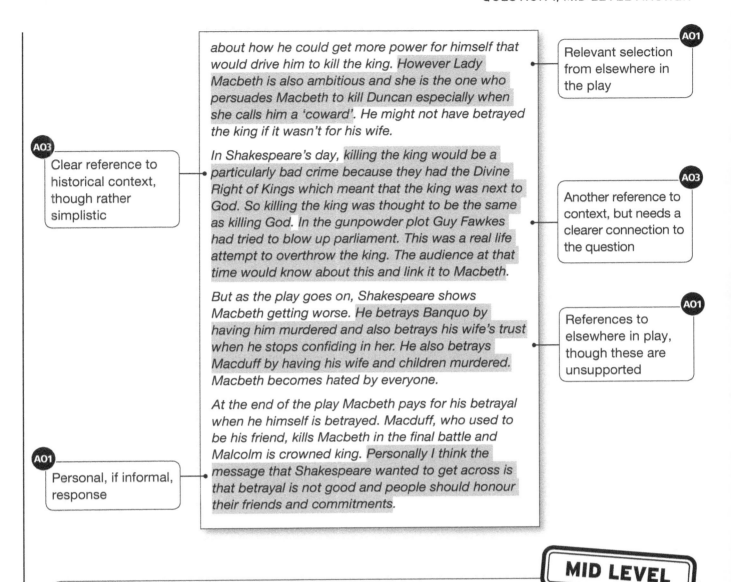

AO1 — Relevant selection from elsewhere in the play

AO3 — Clear reference to historical context, though rather simplistic

AO3 — Another reference to context, but needs a clearer connection to the question

AO1 — References to elsewhere in play, though these are unsupported

AO1 — Personal, if informal, response

about how he could get more power for himself that would drive him to kill the king. However Lady Macbeth is also ambitious and she is the one who persuades Macbeth to kill Duncan especially when she calls him a 'coward'. He might not have betrayed the king if it wasn't for his wife.

In Shakespeare's day, killing the king would be a particularly bad crime because they had the Divine Right of Kings which meant that the king was next to God. So killing the king was thought to be the same as killing God. In the gunpowder plot Guy Fawkes had tried to blow up parliament. This was a real life attempt to overthrow the king. The audience at that time would know about this and link it to Macbeth.

But as the play goes on, Shakespeare shows Macbeth getting worse. He betrays Banquo by having him murdered and also betrays his wife's trust when he stops confiding in her. He also betrays Macduff by having his wife and children murdered. Macbeth becomes hated by everyone.

At the end of the play Macbeth pays for his betrayal when he himself is betrayed. Macduff, who used to be his friend, kills Macbeth in the final battle and Malcolm is crowned king. Personally I think the message that Shakespeare wanted to get across is that betrayal is not good and people should honour their friends and commitments.

MID LEVEL

Comment:
A clear and generally well-structured response, which shows knowledge of the text as a whole. The theme is explored, though at times the points being made could be developed. There is also limited use of literary terminology. There are some useful comments on Shakespeare's language and the overall structure of the play, and quotations are embedded. Appropriate references to historical context are included, though these are a little basic.

For a Good Level:

■ Comment more frequently on how Shakespeare uses language, structure, or aspects such as characters and symbols to convey ideas.

■ Vary the openings of paragraphs.

■ Link all ideas closely to the text, using examples to support answers.

■ Try to include more quotations from other sections of the play and use these to track the way the theme develops.

Sample answer B

AO1 — Relevant quotation from elsewhere in the play

AO2 — Uses literary terminology and explains its effect

AO2 — Clear response to quotation

AO2 — Clear explanation of effect of language

AO4 — Varies sentence structures

AO1 — Good example of a well-chosen single word quotation

Betrayal, where 'fair is foul', is a key theme in 'Macbeth'. In this extract, part of Macbeth's soliloquy from Act I Scene 7, we see him questioning the plot to kill the king. Macbeth talks about how 'innocent' King Duncan is and how it would be 'horrid' to betray him.

This speech is a soliloquy, revealing Macbeth's inner thoughts. Shakespeare uses this technique to show the audience the protagonist's internal struggle. The speech reveals Macbeth's human side and makes him sympathetic as a character. He might be very certain and ruthless on the battlefield, where killing a man is a matter of duty. But this speech reveals that he is not entirely cold-hearted. He does have a conscience and the capacity to doubt. This insight to Macbeth's emotions makes his betrayal of Duncan more unsettling for the audience.

At the start of this extract Macbeth examines his responsibility to the king, who is a guest in Macbeth's castle. Macbeth says that a host should look after his visitors and against 'his murderer shut the door, / Not bear the knife'. This shows that he knows betrayal would be wrong on many levels.

Shakespeare uses this speech to present Duncan as kind and honourable, further intensifying the horror of Macbeth's planned betrayal. Macbeth will kill a good king who 'hath borne his faculties so meek'. The adjective 'meek' reminds us of the Bible where the 'meek shall inherit the earth' and emphasises Duncan's innocence. James I wrote about the Divine Right of Kings, a system in which kings were answerable only to God, suggesting that Macbeth's betrayal would be against both the king and God.

In this extract Macbeth uses euphemisms such as 'horrid deed' and avoids more honest words like 'death, 'murder' or 'kill'. This suggests that he is unwilling, or unable, to face the immensity of the task he intends to undertake. The adjective 'horrid' shows that Macbeth understands how heinous it would be to kill the king. It also shows he feels disturbed by the plan.

Throughout the play Macbeth betrays Banquo, Macduff, and the people of Scotland. He is described as a 'devil' by other characters, which shows that he is associated with hell. In this way, Shakespeare shows Macbeth to be the opposite of the good King Duncan, suggesting that Macbeth's betrayal has led to a reign of terror.

When Macbeth betrays his friend Banquo his motive is paranoia. The witches prophesised that Banquo

AO1 — Clear appreciation of the extract's significance

AO1 — Explanation of character

AO2 — Effect of drama

AO2 — Embedded quotation

AO2 — Builds on previous point

AO3 — Links historical context to play

AO2 — Varied use of subject terminology

AO2 — Selects and explores individual word

AO1 — Refers to rest of play

AO1 — Repetition of 'shows' – a different verb would be preferable

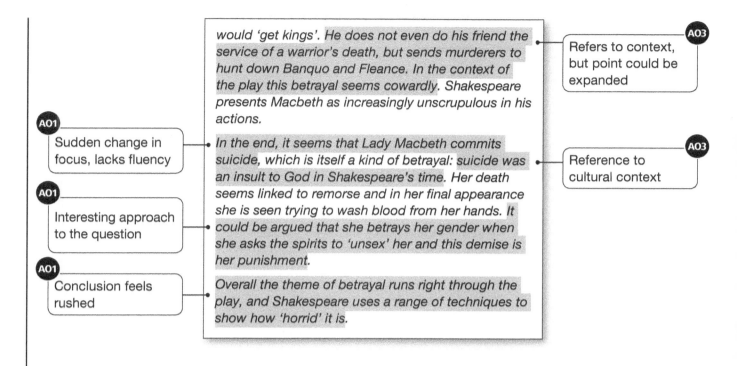

AO3 Refers to context, but point could be expanded

AO3 Reference to cultural context

AO1 Sudden change in focus, lacks fluency

AO1 Interesting approach to the question

AO1 Conclusion feels rushed

> would 'get kings'. He does not even do his friend the service of a warrior's death, but sends murderers to hunt down Banquo and Fleance. In the context of the play this betrayal seems cowardly. Shakespeare presents Macbeth as increasingly unscrupulous in his actions.
>
> In the end, it seems that Lady Macbeth commits suicide, which is itself a kind of betrayal: suicide was an insult to God in Shakespeare's time. Her death seems linked to remorse and in her final appearance she is seen trying to wash blood from her hands. It could be argued that she betrays her gender when she asks the spirits to 'unsex' her and this demise is her punishment.
>
> Overall the theme of betrayal runs right through the play, and Shakespeare uses a range of techniques to show how 'horrid' it is.

GOOD LEVEL

Comment:
This is a sustained and generally fluent response, which is detailed and thoughtful and shows understanding of the whole play. There is evidence of deeper understanding and an ability to interpret ideas. Relevant comments are made on Shakespeare's techniques and their effects, and some good examples are selected from the rest of the play, though these could be examined more closely. There are also some relevant connections made to wider context.

For a High Level:

■ Plan in more depth, considering where points can be linked together.

■ Consider how to further meet AO3 by commenting on the context of the play – this can be literary as well as social.

■ Aim to work at a high level of detail throughout the response.

■ Maintain the fluency of expression to the end.

Sample answer C

AO1 — Relevant reference to literary context

'Macbeth' is a tragedy in which the hero's downfall begins with betrayal, a theme that is central to the play. In the very first scene three witches warn that 'Fair is foul and foul is fair', an incantation that sets the tone for foul-play and treachery. Betrayals range from the first Thane of Cawdor's traitorous behaviour in battle, to Lady Macbeth's betrayal of her gender, and Macbeth's betrayal of the king.

AO4 — Sophisticated vocabulary and expression

AO1 — Highly effective overarching summary of theme in play

AO1 — Refers to elsewhere in play

AO1 — Use of embedded quotations

Prior to this extract, Lady Macbeth has called on 'spirits' to 'unsex' her. She invokes supernatural forces, demanding a masculine strength that could be seen to betray her gender. She accuses her husband, lauded for his fearlessness, of being 'too full o'the milk of human-kindness'. Her ambition leads her to manipulate, and in a sense betray, her husband. She will 'pour [her] spirits in [his] ear' and pushes Macbeth to murder Duncan, to meet her own desire to be queen.

AO1 — Focus on question, with relevant exploration

AO1 — Awareness of writer's craft

In this particular extract, Shakespeare uses a soliloquy to present Macbeth's internal struggle over the proposed betrayal. Earlier in the speech, Macbeth's language is euphemistic: 'If it were done when 'tis done'. Macbeth's use of the pronoun 'it' shows his inability to name the act: 'murder', indicating his discomfort.

AO2 — Effective use of literary terminology

AO2 — Close analysis of language

Through Macbeth, Shakespeare presents Duncan as a paragon of leadership who is 'clear in his great office'. The adjective 'great' suggests both the high calibre of Duncan's rule, and also the importance of the king in society. According to James I's guidebook to sovereignty, 'Basilikon Doron', kings were so significant that 'by God himself they are called gods'. Shakespeare appears to support (or pander to) this view when Macbeth claims Duncan's 'virtues / Will plead like angels', a simile implying Heaven will be distraught at his death. Macbeth acknowledges the seriousness of the assassination plot: he will betray a friend who's 'here in double trust' as the king and, as a consequence, God.

AO2 — Selects individual word to examine

AO3 — Relevant and interesting reference to context

AO1 — Examines layers of meaning in the question

Another of Macbeth's concerns about the betrayal is related to Duncan's innocence. The simile 'like a naked new-born babe' presents an image of defencelessness and purity. The assonance of the long 'a', coupled with the alliteration, suggests wailing or sobbing. Later in this scene Lady Macbeth says she knows 'how tender 'tis to love the babe that milks me', suggesting that the Macbeths have lost a child. These images of babies combine to fill the audience with dread about the assassination plot. They could also, perhaps, suggest an underlying grief in Macbeth, even trauma.

AO1 — Close analysis of language

AO1 — Suitably tentative

AO1 — Well-chosen link to elsewhere in the scene

However, Macbeth admits his only justification for betraying Duncan is his own 'vaulting ambition'. Shakespeare uses a verb as an adjective in 'vaulting' and the effect is to make Macbeth's ambition seem beyond his control, like an untamed horse. This conclusion about his motive stops Macbeth. As his soliloquy continues, he declares: 'We will proceed no further in this business'. However, he soon renounces his decision, betraying himself, when Lady Macbeth accuses him of cowardice.

AO1 — Relevant reference to elsewhere, showing strong overall knowledge

After the murder, the guilt of betrayal disturbs Macbeth. He is now able to utter the word 'murder', but not 'the king' or 'Duncan'. His lamentation 'Macbeth does murder sleep!' shows the immense consequence of betrayal: there will be no rest for Macbeth, his wife, or Scotland.

AO3 — Contextual reference

Later, after the 'terrible feat' and accession to the throne, Macbeth commits further betrayals: he has his fellow soldier Banquo murdered and arranges for Macduff's innocent family to be 'savagely slaughtered'. With these treacherous acts against the blameless and defenceless, Macbeth betrays his own warrior creed.

AO1 — Links evidence from elsewhere in the play back to the extract

Macbeth also betrays his role as leader. Instead of offering protection to Scotland, he rules with violence: he is a 'devil', a 'hell-kite', a 'hell-hound'. With these associations to the underworld, Shakespeare creates a contrast between Macbeth and Duncan as portrayed in the extract.

AO1 — Concise conclusion

In the end the betrayer is betrayed. On an emotional level Macbeth is betrayed by his mind – he is haunted by 'terrible dreams' and 'gory' hallucinations and does not enjoy the power he sought. His 'dearest chuck', Lady Macbeth, descends into madness, a kind of betrayal of marriage – she is no longer able to equal her husband. Finally, Macbeth is betrayed politically by Macduff and Malcolm. This betrayal, if it is one, is simply the usurping of a 'butcher' king, and therefore seems a fair and just final outcome.

VERY HIGH LEVEL

Comment:
A convincing answer which examines various angles of the theme with a range of evidence, from both the extract and the play as a whole. There is a range of knowledge demonstrated, across and beyond the text, which is well articulated and exemplified using well-chosen quotations.

Question 2

Read the following extract from Act II Scene 2 of *Macbeth* and then answer the question that follows.

At this point in the play, Macbeth has just murdered King Duncan.

LADY MACBETH

These deeds must not be thought

After these ways; so, it will make us mad.

MACBETH

Methought I heard a voice cry, 'Sleep no more!

Macbeth does murder sleep – the innocent sleep,

5   Sleep that knits up the ravelled sleave of care,

The death of each day's life, sore labour's bath,

Balm of hurt minds, great nature's second course,

Chief nourisher in life's feast.'

LADY MACBETH

What do you mean?

MACBETH

Still it cried 'Sleep no more' to all the house;

10   'Glamis hath murdered sleep, and therefore Cawdor

Shall sleep no more, Macbeth shall sleep no more.'

Starting with this conversation, explore how Shakespeare presents the theme of sleep.

Write about:

■ how Shakespeare presents the theme of sleep in this conversation

■ how Shakespeare presents the theme of sleep in the play as a whole.

[30 marks]

AO4 [4 marks]

Annotated sample answers

Now, read the three sample answers that follow and, based on what you have read, try to allocate a level to your own work. Which of the three responses is your answer closest to? Don't be discouraged if your work doesn't seem as strong as some of the responses here – the point is to use these samples to learn about what is needed and then put it into practice in your own work. Conversely, you may have mentioned relevant ideas or points that don't appear in these responses; if this is the case, give yourself a pat on the back – it shows you are considering lots of good ideas.

Sample answer A

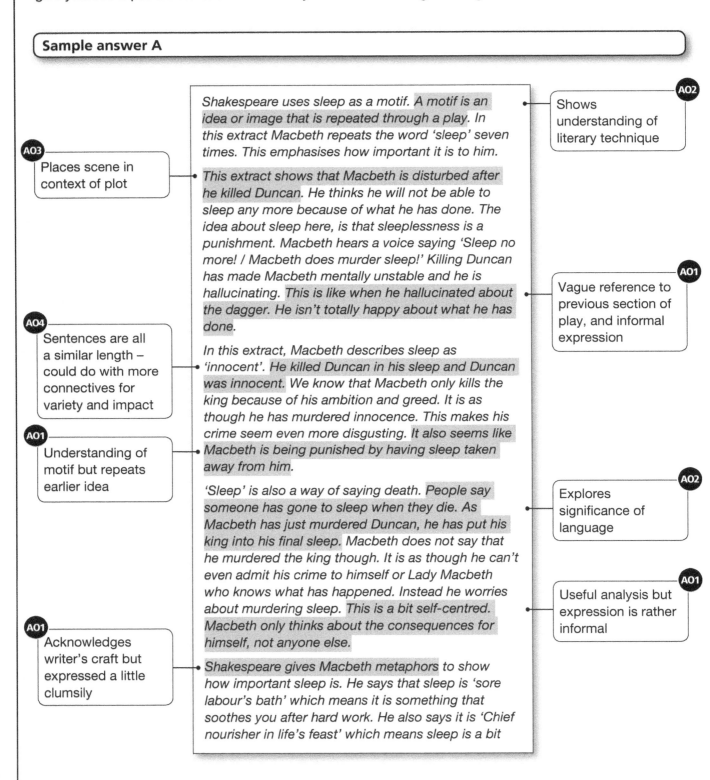

AO2 Shows understanding of literary technique

AO3 Places scene in context of plot

AO1 Vague reference to previous section of play, and informal expression

AO4 Sentences are all a similar length – could do with more connectives for variety and impact

AO1 Understanding of motif but repeats earlier idea

AO2 Explores significance of language

AO1 Useful analysis but expression is rather informal

AO1 Acknowledges writer's craft but expressed a little clumsily

Shakespeare uses sleep as a motif. A motif is an idea or image that is repeated through a play. In this extract Macbeth repeats the word 'sleep' seven times. This emphasises how important it is to him.

This extract shows that Macbeth is disturbed after he killed Duncan. He thinks he will not be able to sleep any more because of what he has done. The idea about sleep here, is that sleeplessness is a punishment. Macbeth hears a voice saying 'Sleep no more! / Macbeth does murder sleep!' Killing Duncan has made Macbeth mentally unstable and he is hallucinating. This is like when he hallucinated about the dagger. He isn't totally happy about what he has done.

In this extract, Macbeth describes sleep as 'innocent'. He killed Duncan in his sleep and Duncan was innocent. We know that Macbeth only kills the king because of his ambition and greed. It is as though he has murdered innocence. This makes his crime seem even more disgusting. It also seems like Macbeth is being punished by having sleep taken away from him.

'Sleep' is also a way of saying death. People say someone has gone to sleep when they die. As Macbeth has just murdered Duncan, he has put his king into his final sleep. Macbeth does not say that he murdered the king though. It is as though he can't even admit his crime to himself or Lady Macbeth who knows what has happened. Instead he worries about murdering sleep. This is a bit self-centred. Macbeth only thinks about the consequences for himself, not anyone else.

Shakespeare gives Macbeth metaphors to show how important sleep is. He says that sleep is 'sore labour's bath' which means it is something that soothes you after hard work. He also says it is 'Chief nourisher in life's feast' which means sleep is a bit

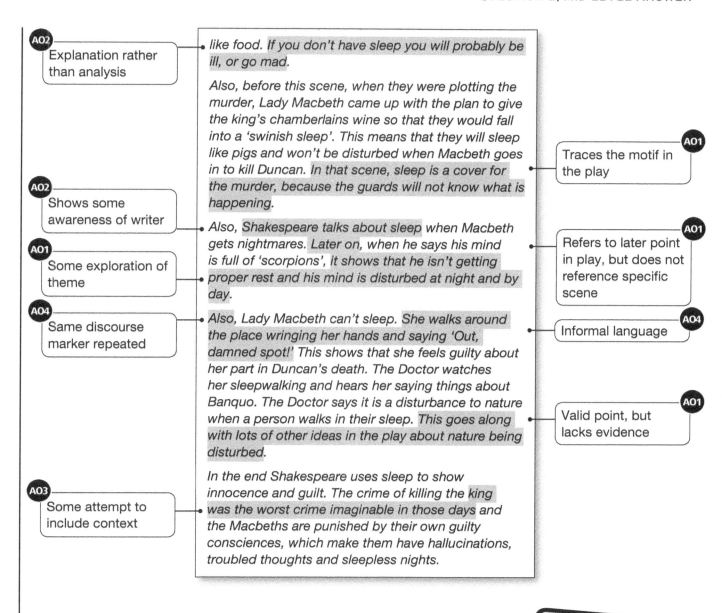

AO2 Explanation rather than analysis

AO2 Shows some awareness of writer

AO1 Some exploration of theme

AO4 Same discourse marker repeated

AO3 Some attempt to include context

like food. *If you don't have sleep you will probably be ill, or go mad.*

Also, before this scene, when they were plotting the murder, Lady Macbeth came up with the plan to give the king's chamberlains wine so that they would fall into a 'swinish sleep'. This means that they will sleep like pigs and won't be disturbed when Macbeth goes in to kill Duncan. In that scene, sleep is a cover for the murder, because the guards will not know what is happening.

Also, Shakespeare talks about sleep when Macbeth gets nightmares. Later on, when he says his mind is full of 'scorpions', it shows that he isn't getting proper rest and his mind is disturbed at night and by day.

Also, Lady Macbeth can't sleep. She walks around the place wringing her hands and saying 'Out, damned spot!' This shows that she feels guilty about her part in Duncan's death. The Doctor watches her sleepwalking and hears her saying things about Banquo. The Doctor says it is a disturbance to nature when a person walks in their sleep. This goes along with lots of other ideas in the play about nature being disturbed.

In the end Shakespeare uses sleep to show innocence and guilt. The crime of killing the king was the worst crime imaginable in those days and the Macbeths are punished by their own guilty consciences, which make them have hallucinations, troubled thoughts and sleepless nights.

AO1 Traces the motif in the play

AO1 Refers to later point in play, but does not reference specific scene

AO4 Informal language

AO1 Valid point, but lacks evidence

MID LEVEL

Comment:
This is a focused response to the question that explains ideas and points clearly and logically. Quotations are generally relevant and support what is being said, though more in-depth analysis would be useful. Shows some understanding of the writer's techniques, but reference to context is limited.

For a Good Level:

- Include more relevant and precise contextual support.
- Analyse language from the extract in closer detail.
- Examine the layers of meaning in particular words.
- Aim to include more literary terminology.
- Express ideas more fluently with a greater variety of sentences.

Sample answer B

This scene presents a key motif in 'Macbeth': sleep. Shakespeare uses the concept of sleep throughout the play – the word itself appears thirty-two times in total. Sleep is used to represent innocence, peace of mind and the natural cycle of life. Sleep is a 'nourisher' and important for good health. In this scene, Macbeth is worried that he has murdered sleep, showing that his murder of Duncan has disturbing implications.

AO1 — Confident, detailed introduction

Before the scene this extract comes from, the idea of 'sleep' appears with Lady Macbeth's plot to take advantage of sleep by plying the king's guards with wine, sending them to 'swinish sleep'. The word 'swinish' shows that the guards will be like pigs, grunting in ignorant wine-drenched sleep. Their sleep will be the cover under which Macbeth will murder the king, so sleep is useful to the Macbeths at this point.

AO1 — Well-embedded quotation

AO1 — Picks out individual word but needs to choose words that relate more closely to the theme

Before the murder, Banquo experiences troubled sleep. He meets Macbeth late at night, saying, 'What, sir, not yet at rest?' Banquo doesn't know that Macbeth is about to kill Duncan, so his question makes a link with this extract, which comes after the murder. Here, Macbeth imagines a voice crying, 'Macbeth does murder sleep!'. The voice embodies Macbeth's paranoia and fear. He will never be 'at rest' again.

AO4 — Similar opening to previous paragraph

AO2 — Links quotations from different parts of play

It is ironic that Macbeth worries about a lack of sleep when he has just killed Duncan in his sleep. It is Duncan who will not sleep – or wake – any more. To any audience, murdering someone in their sleep would seem dreadful, but it was even worse at the time Shakespeare was writing about. In medieval Scotland, the king was the head of everything and to kill him showed disregard for the whole country.

AO2 — Apt use of literary term

AO3 — Includes context, though could explore this further

The cry 'Macbeth does murder sleep' shows that Macbeth is disturbed by his actions. He feels horrified and thinks he will be haunted by guilt and nightmares forever. Sleep, therefore, could be said to represent innocence. It suggests Duncan's innocence and could also refer to the innocence of the people like Banquo, and Macduff's children, who Macbeth will go on to kill.

AO2 — Examines significance of key word

Macbeth also refers to sleep as 'the death of each day's life'. This metaphor shows how the natural order of things should go through cycles: day and night, life and death, summer and winter. Macbeth realises that he has disrupted the natural order of everything and that he will suffer by no longer being able to rest.

AO4 — Uses literary terminology appropriately

AO1 — Clear explanation of effect

Macbeth describes sleep as a 'chief nourisher'. A lack of sleep means a lack of nourishment, which leads to sickness. This links to Lady Macbeth's

AO2 — Begins to analyse language, though could go deeper

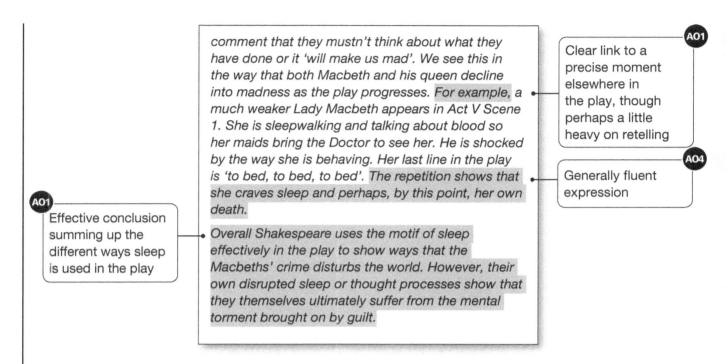

comment that they mustn't think about what they have done or it 'will make us mad'. We see this in the way that both Macbeth and his queen decline into madness as the play progresses. For example, a much weaker Lady Macbeth appears in Act V Scene 1. She is sleepwalking and talking about blood so her maids bring the Doctor to see her. He is shocked by the way she is behaving. Her last line in the play is 'to bed, to bed, to bed'. The repetition shows that she craves sleep and perhaps, by this point, her own death.

Overall Shakespeare uses the motif of sleep effectively in the play to show ways that the Macbeths' crime disturbs the world. However, their own disrupted sleep or thought processes show that they themselves ultimately suffer from the mental torment brought on by guilt.

AO1 Clear link to a precise moment elsewhere in the play, though perhaps a little heavy on retelling

AO4 Generally fluent expression

AO1 Effective conclusion summing up the different ways sleep is used in the play

GOOD LEVEL

Comment:
This is solid, fluent and well argued, with embedded quotations throughout. There is increasing evidence of deeper understanding and an ability to interpret ideas. Shows a good understanding of the way Shakespeare uses 'sleep' as a motif throughout the play as a whole.

For a High Level:

- Aim to analyse key words and phrases in more detail.
- Look for subtleties of meaning and examine less obvious significance of words.
- Find further opportunities to incorporate historical and social context.

Sample answer C

AO2 — Appropriate use of terminology

AO2 — Relevant embedded quotation

AO1 — Explores layers of meaning

AO1 — Fluent linking and expression of ideas

AO1 — Strong control of language and effective repetition

Shakespeare uses the motif of sleep throughout 'Macbeth', starting in Act I Scene 3 when the witches cast a spell on a sailor to prevent him from sleeping. This foreshadows the Macbeths' experiences of sleeplessness following the murder of Duncan. It also foreshadows the way that sleep represents innocence, and that its opposite, sleeplessness, here conjured by the forces of evil, signifies corruption.

In the given extract, the 'deed' has been done. Macbeth has killed the king, a crime even more awful in the medieval context of the play when the king held a patriarchal position. King Duncan is the 'Lord's anointed temple', central on a spiritual as well as a political level. James I wrote about the Divine Right of Kings, suggesting that a king was the head of a 'microcosm of the body of man'. Macbeth's action disturbs the natural order and is therefore an offence to God. When he hallucinates and imagines a voice crying, 'Sleep no more! / Macbeth does murder sleep', it implies that the peace of mind that comes with sleep, and perhaps prayer, has been destroyed. It also suggests that all hopes for a peaceful Scotland have gone.

In addition, the use of the present tense form 'does' implies that Macbeth is unable to clear his mind of what he has done. Mentally he is still murdering Duncan. The word 'does' also refers back to Act I Scene 7, when Lady Macbeth taunted her husband saying 'When you durst do it, then you were a man.' Now he 'does' it but the outcome is sleepless torture. Sleep is 'the death of each day's life' and without it, there is a continuous and hellish present, a mental disturbance that makes both Lady Macbeth and her husband 'mad'.

In fact, Macbeth is already in a state of hysteria. He manically repeats the word 'sleep', implying horror at his actions, and a wish that he could become unconscious of what he has done.

This hysteria is also seen in the way in which Macbeth babbles a list of metaphors that show the benefits of sleep. It brings peace of mind and 'knits up the ravelled sleave of care'. It soothes physical and emotional wounds through being 'sore labour's bath' and the 'balm of hurt minds'. Shakespeare highlights all the benefits of sleep to emphasise the intensity of Macbeth's punishment: a sleepless life unsoothed and in constant pain. Sleep is the 'Great nourisher'. The adjective 'great' suggests something godly or spiritual. Without sleep, the soul goes unfed.

AO1 — Clear and concise introduction

AO3 — Useful reference to context

AO2 — Close analysis of language

AO1 — Shows secure understanding of play

AO2 — Shows understanding of character

AO2 — Thoughtful examination of individual word

AO2 — Explores wider significance of language

AO3 — Uses context

AO2 — Good understanding of literary techniques

AO1 — Well-rounded argument

Macbeth also recounts how the voice 'cried "Sleep no more!" to all the house'. *The imperative is indisputable: there will be no rest for anyone. The 'house' suggests the Macbeths' home, and could also represent the country. The command is a warning to Scotland to be vigilant.*

Later, in Act III, Macbeth reports 'terrible dreams / That shake us nightly'. *His sleepless paranoia is surely part of what leads him to have Banquo murdered. It is also possible that murdering Banquo is strategic* – Macbeth has invited Banquo to support him and Banquo has rejected the offer. The appearance of Banquo's ghost shaking his 'gory locks' at the feast is nightmarish, and the march of Birnam Wood and the man 'not born of woman' are also so strange as to seem dreamlike. *Macbeth's waking world becomes as awful and surreal as a nightmare.*

Another aspect of sleep which Shakespeare explores in the play is its association with night, a time when primitive fears and insecurities surface, and also one linked to contemporary ideas about the supernatural. The Macbeths' sleeplessness makes them nocturnal creatures and connects them even more closely with evil.

The sleep motif continues in Act V with Lady Macbeth's sleepwalking. Her bedchamber forms a parallel to Duncan's. *Though where Duncan's represents peace, hers is a microcosm of 'perturbation'.* Both rooms witness violence – one in the form of 'gash'd stabs' and the other a violent mental disturbance. *In each, sleep is murdered.*

Finally, Shakespeare combines the *motif of sleep with the motif of blood,* showing Lady Macbeth's mental and emotional breakdown in her sleeping obsession with a 'damned spot' of blood that she cannot wash away. Both the blood and her disturbed sleep represent her guilt and the impossibility of avoiding it. *The motif ends with Lady Macbeth's 'to bed, to bed, to bed' implying her downfall – her deathbed, perhaps, – and pre-empting Macbeth's own descent.*

AO4 — Confident expression and wide vocabulary

AO1 — Excellent use of critical style, honing the argument

AO1 — Examines motif in detail

AO4 — Very high level use of relevant vocabulary

AO1 — Explores parallels

VERY HIGH LEVEL

Comment:
A sustained and convincing answer which presents a wide range of evidence from the extract and across the play as a whole. Knowledge of the theme, and how it is presented across and beyond the text is articulated strongly and exemplified using well-chosen quotations, and detailed analysis.

Question 3

Read the following extract from Act I Scene 2 of *Macbeth* and then answer the question that follows.

At this point in the play, the Captain is describing to King Duncan what has happened on the battlefield.

> **MALCOLM**
>
> Say to the king the knowledge of the broil
> As thou didst leave it.
>
> **CAPTAIN**
>
>   Doubtful it stood,
> As two spent swimmers, that do cling together
> And choke their art. The merciless Macdonwald –
> 5   Worthy to be a rebel, for to that
> The multiplying villainies of nature
> Do swarm upon him – from the Western Isles
> Of kerns and galloglasses is supplied,
> And fortune on his damnèd quarrel smiling
> 10 Showed like a rebel's whore. But all's too weak:
> For brave Macbeth – well he deserves that name –
> Disdaining fortune, with his brandished steel,
> Which smoked with bloody execution,
> Like valour's minion carvèd out his passage
> 15 Till he faced the slave –
> Which ne'er shook hands nor bade farewell to him
> Till he unseamed him from the nave to the chops,
> And fixed his head upon our battlements.
>
> **KING DUNCAN**
>
> O valiant cousin! Worthy gentleman!

'Shakespeare presents Macbeth as a brave warrior who is worthy of respect.'

Starting with this conversation, explore how far you agree with this opinion.

Write about:

- how far Shakespeare presents Macbeth as a brave warrior worthy of respect at this moment in the play
- how far Shakespeare presents Macbeth as a brave warrior worthy of respect in the play as a whole.

[30 marks]

AO4 [4 marks]

Annotated sample answers

Now, read the three sample answers that follow and, based on what you have read, try to allocate a level to your own work. Which of the three responses is your answer closest to? Don't be discouraged if your work doesn't seem as strong as some of the responses here – the point is to use these samples to learn about what is needed and then put it into practice in your own work. Conversely, you may have mentioned relevant ideas or points that don't appear in these responses; if this is the case, give yourself a pat on the back – it shows you are considering lots of good ideas.

Sample answer A

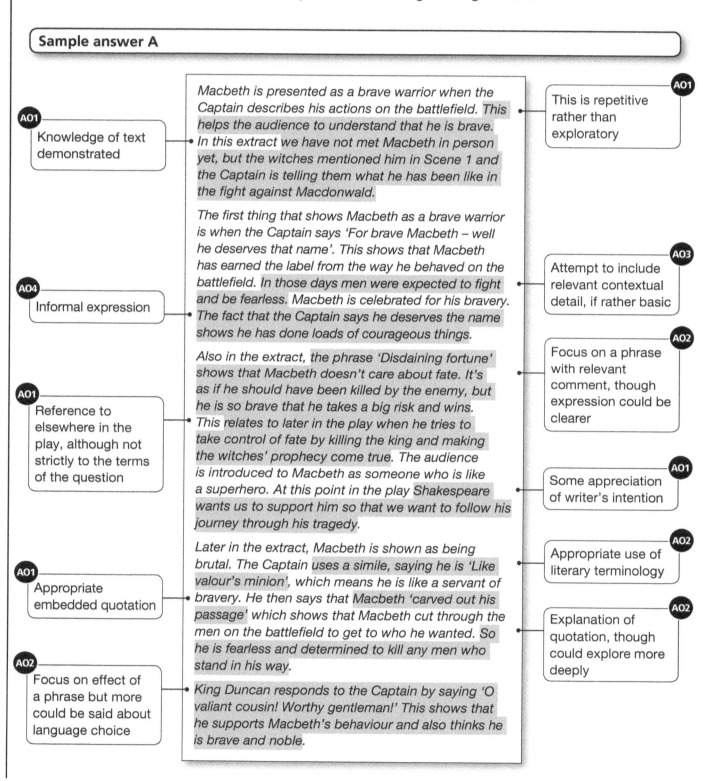

AO1 Knowledge of text demonstrated

AO4 Informal expression

AO1 Reference to elsewhere in the play, although not strictly to the terms of the question

AO1 Appropriate embedded quotation

AO2 Focus on effect of a phrase but more could be said about language choice

Macbeth is presented as a brave warrior when the Captain describes his actions on the battlefield. This helps the audience to understand that he is brave. In this extract we have not met Macbeth in person yet, but the witches mentioned him in Scene 1 and the Captain is telling them what he has been like in the fight against Macdonwald.

The first thing that shows Macbeth as a brave warrior is when the Captain says 'For brave Macbeth – well he deserves that name'. This shows that Macbeth has earned the label from the way he behaved on the battlefield. In those days men were expected to fight and be fearless. Macbeth is celebrated for his bravery. The fact that the Captain says he deserves the name shows he has done loads of courageous things.

Also in the extract, the phrase 'Disdaining fortune' shows that Macbeth doesn't care about fate. It's as if he should have been killed by the enemy, but he is so brave that he takes a big risk and wins. This relates to later in the play when he tries to take control of fate by killing the king and making the witches' prophecy come true. The audience is introduced to Macbeth as someone who is like a superhero. At this point in the play Shakespeare wants us to support him so that we want to follow his journey through his tragedy.

Later in the extract, Macbeth is shown as being brutal. The Captain uses a simile, saying he is 'Like valour's minion', which means he is like a servant of bravery. He then says that Macbeth 'carved out his passage' which shows that Macbeth cut through the men on the battlefield to get to who he wanted. So he is fearless and determined to kill any men who stand in his way.

King Duncan responds to the Captain by saying 'O valiant cousin! Worthy gentleman!' This shows that he supports Macbeth's behaviour and also thinks he is brave and noble.

AO1 This is repetitive rather than exploratory

AO3 Attempt to include relevant contextual detail, if rather basic

AO2 Focus on a phrase with relevant comment, though expression could be clearer

AO1 Some appreciation of writer's intention

AO2 Appropriate use of literary terminology

AO2 Explanation of quotation, though could explore more deeply

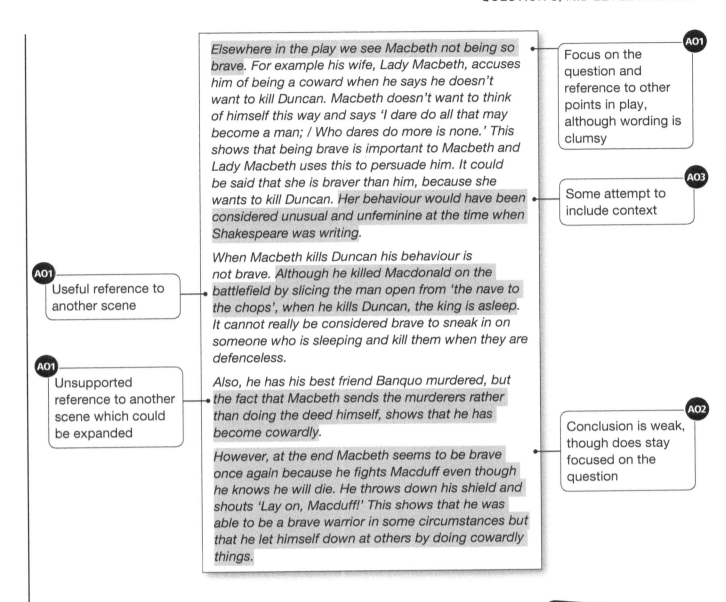

AO1 — Focus on the question and reference to other points in play, although wording is clumsy

Elsewhere in the play we see Macbeth not being so brave. For example his wife, Lady Macbeth, accuses him of being a coward when he says he doesn't want to kill Duncan. Macbeth doesn't want to think of himself this way and says 'I dare do all that may become a man; / Who dares do more is none.' This shows that being brave is important to Macbeth and Lady Macbeth uses this to persuade him. It could be said that she is braver than him, because she wants to kill Duncan. *Her behaviour would have been considered unusual and unfeminine at the time when Shakespeare was writing.*

AO3 — Some attempt to include context

AO1 — Useful reference to another scene

When Macbeth kills Duncan his behaviour is not brave. Although he killed Macdonald on the battlefield by slicing the man open from 'the nave to the chops', when he kills Duncan, the king is asleep. It cannot really be considered brave to sneak in on someone who is sleeping and kill them when they are defenceless.

AO1 — Unsupported reference to another scene which could be expanded

Also, he has his best friend Banquo murdered, but the fact that Macbeth sends the murderers rather than doing the deed himself, shows that he has become cowardly.

AO2 — Conclusion is weak, though does stay focused on the question

However, at the end Macbeth seems to be brave once again because he fights Macduff even though he knows he will die. He throws down his shield and shouts 'Lay on, Macduff!' This shows that he was able to be a brave warrior in some circumstances but that he let himself down at others by doing cowardly things.

MID LEVEL

Comment:
A mostly clear answer which demonstrates knowledge of the play and some good understanding of the way Shakespeare uses the characters. Quotations are usually well chosen, embedded and of appropriate length. Points are mostly focused on the question, although the use of the word 'brave' becomes quite repetitive. There are some comments on the effects of language, although there is listing of events rather than analysis in places. There are some basic comments on social context and its effect on the text.

For a Good Level:

- Expand the range of vocabulary.
- Comment on language, form and structure more frequently, e.g. by labelling techniques used in quotations and examining their effect.
- Make more effective links between the context and the text.

Sample answer B

AO1 Shows knowledge of the text by placing the extract in context

AO1 Shows appreciation of writer's intention

Shakespeare uses various techniques to present Macbeth as a brave warrior. One of these is to paint a picture of him through other people's eyes, and this is what happens in this extract which comes at the very start of the play, before we have even met the protagonist. This creates expectation for the audience. Shakespeare makes us wait to meet this man who has shown such fearlessness on the battlefield.

AO2 Embeds quotation well

In this extract the Captain describes Macbeth's behaviour on the battlefield. He explains how 'brave Macbeth' fought with determination and single-minded focus. The outcome of the battle seemed 'doubtful' with both sides as weary as 'two spent swimmers', but Macbeth 'like valour's minion carved out his passage' to the enemy Macdonwald. This simile shows that Macbeth is a servant to bravery, as though his sole purpose is to commit acts of intrepid heroism. The verb 'carved' is unsettling because it refers to cutting up human beings. So, the audience might feel awe, but also fear towards Macbeth.

AO2 Uses literary term and explores significance

AO2 Closer examination of effects of language

This feeling is increased when the Captain describes how Macbeth killed Macdonwald: he 'unseamed him from the nave to the chops'. This shows how Macbeth sliced his enemy open and implies that he is brave, but also brutal. He is capable of extreme acts of violence. This was considered an asset in the medieval setting of the play, when men fought with fists and steel to defend their kingdoms. The ability to act boldly like Macbeth was thought of as a strength.

AO4 Increasingly confident expression

AO3 Appropriate reference to context

Duncan celebrates Macbeth and shows his admiration for the warrior-hero when he exclaims 'O, valiant cousin! Worthy gentleman!' However this contrasts with the way Macbeth acts towards Duncan later in the play. Macbeth and his wife plot to kill the 'unguarded Duncan' and murder him in his sleep. Not surprisingly, this act of violence is not celebrated, and marks the turning point for Macbeth. Shakespeare shows how the 'brave' warrior is driven by his 'vaulting ambition' (and his persuasive wife) to commit atrocities.

AO1 Relevant link to elsewhere – showing clear comparison

AO1 Shows understanding of structure

AO1 Shows knowledge of the text as a whole

From this point Macbeth's behaviour is increasingly cowardly. The play is a tragedy, which means we expect to follow the hero to his downfall. But this hero is one whose actions are unheroic. After he kills his king, Macbeth is tormented by paranoia and fear, hardly evidence of courage. He recruits murderers to kill his friend Banquo and Banquo's son Fleance rather than do it himself. When Banquo's ghost

AO3 Understanding of literary context

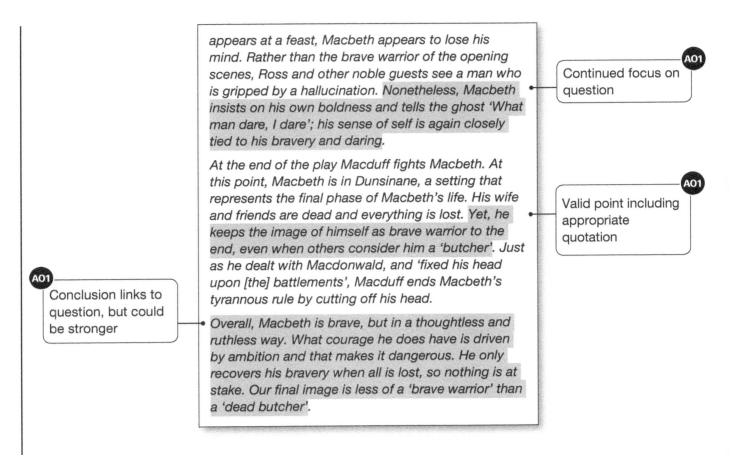

appears at a feast, Macbeth appears to lose his mind. Rather than the brave warrior of the opening scenes, Ross and other noble guests see a man who is gripped by a hallucination. Nonetheless, Macbeth insists on his own boldness and tells the ghost 'What man dare, I dare'; his sense of self is again closely tied to his bravery and daring.

At the end of the play Macduff fights Macbeth. At this point, Macbeth is in Dunsinane, a setting that represents the final phase of Macbeth's life. His wife and friends are dead and everything is lost. Yet, he keeps the image of himself as brave warrior to the end, even when others consider him a 'butcher'. Just as he dealt with Macdonwald, and 'fixed his head upon [the] battlements', Macduff ends Macbeth's tyrannous rule by cutting off his head.

Overall, Macbeth is brave, but in a thoughtless and ruthless way. What courage he does have is driven by ambition and that makes it dangerous. He only recovers his bravery when all is lost, so nothing is at stake. Our final image is less of a 'brave warrior' than a 'dead butcher'.

AO1 Continued focus on question

AO1 Valid point including appropriate quotation

AO1 Conclusion links to question, but could be stronger

GOOD LEVEL

Comment:
This is a competent answer which draws ideas from the whole text and makes links between the rest of the play and the extract effectively. It refers to the play's context at times and begins to discuss Macbeth's character. There is some analysis of Shakespeare's language choices and literary terminology is used to discuss these in some detail.

For a High Level:

- Aim to include a wider range of references and quotations.
- Develop comments on context and link them more explicitly to language, form or structure.
- Consider making fewer different points to allow for more analytical depth.

Sample answer C

AO1 Strong opening that responds to the question

Although we are yet to meet Macbeth, Shakespeare establishes him as a brave and ruthless warrior in Act I Scene 2. This effect is created when the Captain describes Macbeth's fearless actions on the battlefield, showing how 'brave Macbeth' lets nothing stand between him and his enemy. Shakespeare introduces a warrior hero, preparing the way for the tragic downfall of a man whose deeds are initially perceived as 'valiant' and 'worthy' as well as 'brave'.

From the start, Macbeth is linked to verbs of violence: 'brandished', 'smoked', 'carved', 'unseamed'. This is a man of fearless action. Shakespeare builds expectation in the audience, making them anticipate with awe and trepidation the entrance of the play's protagonist.

AO2 Convincing explanation

AO2 Linguistic terminology

AO1 Well-selected, embedded quotations

In this extract we learn that the outcome of the battle was 'doubtful' until Macbeth, 'disdaining fortune', made his way through 'like valour's minion' to destroy Macdonwald. The simile aligns Macbeth with courage in a way that makes him seem at the mercy of his own boldness. The way Macbeth's sword 'smoked with bloody execution' lends a supernatural air to his appearance. The verb 'carved' implies that Macbeth's brutality is effortless. There is a ruthlessness to his bravery.

AO2 Embedded quotation with explanation

AO2 Appropriate literary terminology and effect

AO2 Concise explanation of effect of language

This is also shown by Macbeth's violent treatment of his enemy. He did not simply kill Macdonwald, he 'unseamed him from the nave to the chops', suggesting an unflinching ferocity. The verb 'unseamed' suggests an ease to the violence, as though Macbeth's sword has pulled the other man's body apart as simply as tearing cloth. However, this might also be a very early hint of the way Macbeth becomes 'unseamed' as the play progresses. Modern audiences might even wonder if all this experience of violence has desensitised him to it.

AO4 Confident use of different sentence structures

AO3 Interesting link to modern context

AO1 Refers to rest of the play

In traditional medieval fashion, he 'fixed [Macdonwald's] head upon our battlements', a threatening display of strength to the enemy that foreshadows Macbeth's own death. Yet while we might question this brutality, it could be argued that Macbeth only acts according to the expectations of his day. Bravery in battle was the way a warrior progressed along his career path.

AO3 Appreciation of social context

AO1 Links this scene to later scenes

In this extract Shakespeare uses imagery to paint Macbeth as a larger-than-life protagonist. He stands out in the battlefield and seems ultimately

AO1 Clear about writer's role

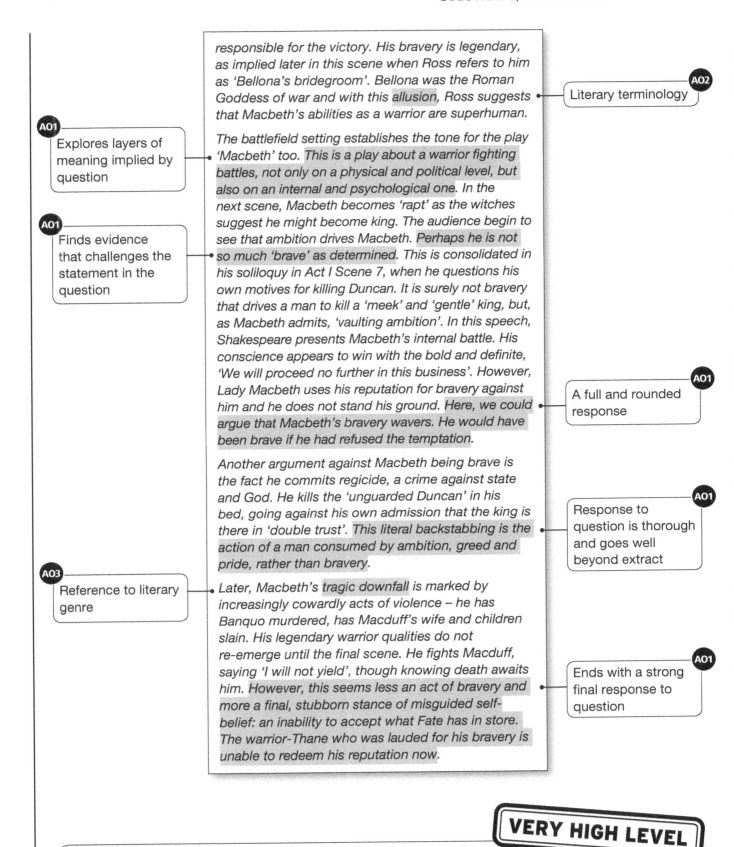

AO1
Explores layers of meaning implied by question

AO1
Finds evidence that challenges the statement in the question

AO3
Reference to literary genre

responsible for the victory. His bravery is legendary, as implied later in this scene when Ross refers to him as 'Bellona's bridegroom'. Bellona was the Roman Goddess of war and with this allusion, Ross suggests that Macbeth's abilities as a warrior are superhuman.

The battlefield setting establishes the tone for the play 'Macbeth' too. This is a play about a warrior fighting battles, not only on a physical and political level, but also on an internal and psychological one. In the next scene, Macbeth becomes 'rapt' as the witches suggest he might become king. The audience begin to see that ambition drives Macbeth. Perhaps he is not so much 'brave' as determined. This is consolidated in his soliloquy in Act I Scene 7, when he questions his own motives for killing Duncan. It is surely not bravery that drives a man to kill a 'meek' and 'gentle' king, but, as Macbeth admits, 'vaulting ambition'. In this speech, Shakespeare presents Macbeth's internal battle. His conscience appears to win with the bold and definite, 'We will proceed no further in this business'. However, Lady Macbeth uses his reputation for bravery against him and he does not stand his ground. Here, we could argue that Macbeth's bravery wavers. He would have been brave if he had refused the temptation.

Another argument against Macbeth being brave is the fact he commits regicide, a crime against state and God. He kills the 'unguarded Duncan' in his bed, going against his own admission that the king is there in 'double trust'. This literal backstabbing is the action of a man consumed by ambition, greed and pride, rather than bravery.

Later, Macbeth's tragic downfall is marked by increasingly cowardly acts of violence – he has Banquo murdered, has Macduff's wife and children slain. His legendary warrior qualities do not re-emerge until the final scene. He fights Macduff, saying 'I will not yield', though knowing death awaits him. However, this seems less an act of bravery and more a final, stubborn stance of misguided self-belief: an inability to accept what Fate has in store. The warrior-Thane who was lauded for his bravery is unable to redeem his reputation now.

AO2
Literary terminology

AO1
A full and rounded response

AO1
Response to question is thorough and goes well beyond extract

AO1
Ends with a strong final response to question

VERY HIGH LEVEL

Comment:
This response shows a highly confident understanding of the text as a whole. The use of references and quotations is well judged and wide-ranging. Comments on the writers' use of language, form and structure are focused on finely-tuned details. The writing is convincing and relevant throughout.

Question 4

Read the following extract from Act I Scene 7 of *Macbeth* and then answer the question that follows.

At this point in the play, Lady Macbeth and Macbeth are discussing the plan to murder Duncan.

> **MACBETH**
> We will proceed no further in this business.
> He hath honoured me of late, and I have bought
> Golden opinions from all sorts of people
> Which would be worn now in their newest gloss,
> 5   Not cast aside so soon.
> **LADY MACBETH**
>   Was the hope drunk
> Wherein you dressed yourself? Hath it slept since?
> And wakes it now, to look so green and pale
> At what it did so freely? From this time
> Such I account thy love. Art thou afeard
> 10   To be the same in thine own act and valour
> As thou art in desire? Wouldst thou have that
> Which thou esteem'st the ornament of life,
> And live a coward in thine own esteem,
> Letting 'I dare not' wait upon 'I would',
> 15   Like the poor cat i' the adage?
> **MACBETH**
>   Prithee peace.
> I dare do all that may become a man;
> Who dares do more is none.
> **LADY MACBETH**
>   What beast was't then
> That made you break this enterprise to me?
> When you durst do it, then you were a man;
> 20   And to be more than what you were, you would
> Be so much more the man.

Starting with this conversation, write about how Shakespeare presents the relationship between Macbeth and Lady Macbeth.

Write about:

- how far Shakespeare presents the relationship in this conversation
- how far Shakespeare presents the relationship in the play as a whole.

[30 marks]
AO4 [4 marks]

Annotated sample answers

Now, read the three sample answers that follow and, based on what you have read, try to allocate a level to your own work. Which of the three responses is your answer closest to? Don't be discouraged if your work doesn't seem as strong as some of the responses here – the point is to use these samples to learn about what is needed and then put it into practice in your own work. Conversely, you may have mentioned relevant ideas or points that don't appear in these responses; if this is the case, give yourself a pat on the back – it shows you are considering lots of good ideas.

Sample answer A

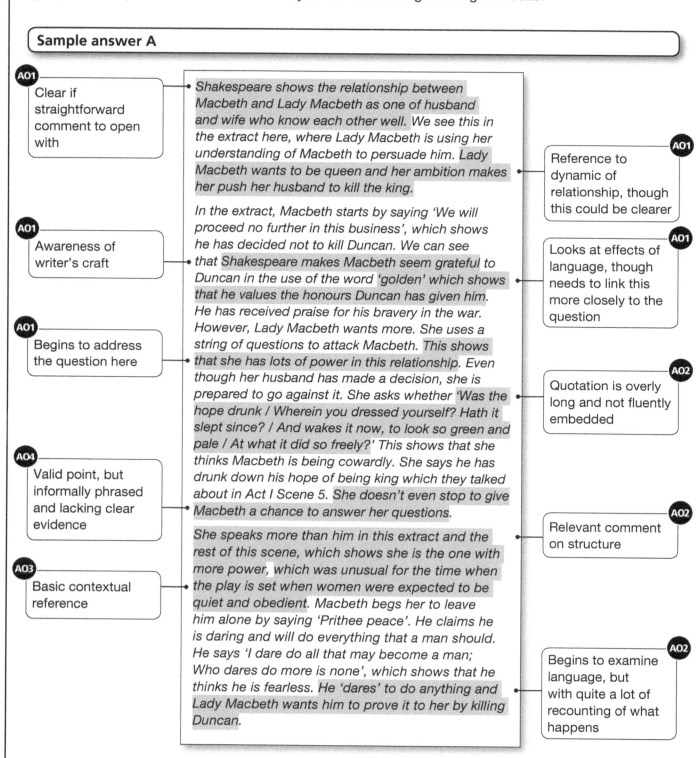

AO1 — Clear if straightforward comment to open with

AO1 — Awareness of writer's craft

AO1 — Begins to address the question here

AO4 — Valid point, but informally phrased and lacking clear evidence

AO3 — Basic contextual reference

Shakespeare shows the relationship between Macbeth and Lady Macbeth as one of husband and wife who know each other well. We see this in the extract here, where Lady Macbeth is using her understanding of Macbeth to persuade him. Lady Macbeth wants to be queen and her ambition makes her push her husband to kill the king.

In the extract, Macbeth starts by saying 'We will proceed no further in this business', which shows he has decided not to kill Duncan. We can see that Shakespeare makes Macbeth seem grateful to Duncan in the use of the word 'golden' which shows that he values the honours Duncan has given him. He has received praise for his bravery in the war. However, Lady Macbeth wants more. She uses a string of questions to attack Macbeth. This shows that she has lots of power in this relationship. Even though her husband has made a decision, she is prepared to go against it. She asks whether 'Was the hope drunk / Wherein you dressed yourself? Hath it slept since? / And wakes it now, to look so green and pale / At what it did so freely?' This shows that she thinks Macbeth is being cowardly. She says he has drunk down his hope of being king which they talked about in Act I Scene 5. She doesn't even stop to give Macbeth a chance to answer her questions.

She speaks more than him in this extract and the rest of this scene, which shows she is the one with more power, which was unusual for the time when the play is set when women were expected to be quiet and obedient. Macbeth begs her to leave him alone by saying 'Prithee peace'. He claims he is daring and will do everything that a man should. He says 'I dare do all that may become a man; Who dares do more is none', which shows that he thinks he is fearless. He 'dares' to do anything and Lady Macbeth wants him to prove it to her by killing Duncan.

AO1 — Reference to dynamic of relationship, though this could be clearer

AO1 — Looks at effects of language, though needs to link this more closely to the question

AO2 — Quotation is overly long and not fluently embedded

AO2 — Relevant comment on structure

AO2 — Begins to examine language, but with quite a lot of recounting of what happens

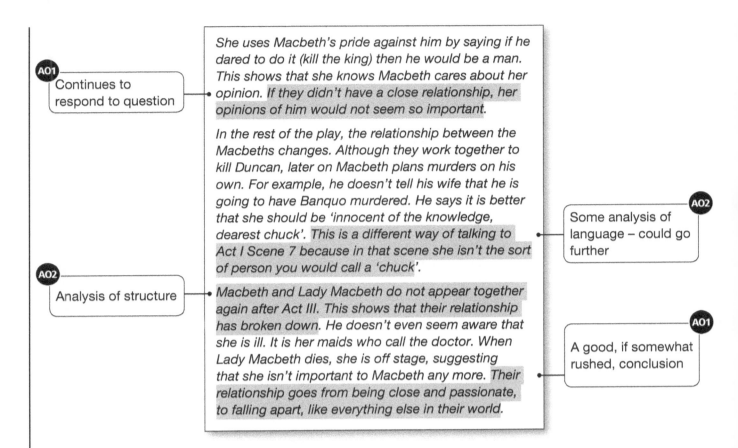

AO1 Continues to respond to question

She uses Macbeth's pride against him by saying if he dared to do it (kill the king) then he would be a man. This shows that she knows Macbeth cares about her opinion. *If they didn't have a close relationship, her opinions of him would not seem so important.*

In the rest of the play, the relationship between the Macbeths changes. Although they work together to kill Duncan, later on Macbeth plans murders on his own. For example, he doesn't tell his wife that he is going to have Banquo murdered. He says it is better that she should be 'innocent of the knowledge, dearest chuck'. *This is a different way of talking to Act I Scene 7 because in that scene she isn't the sort of person you would call a 'chuck'.*

AO2 Some analysis of language – could go further

AO2 Analysis of structure

Macbeth and Lady Macbeth do not appear together again after Act III. This shows that their relationship has broken down. He doesn't even seem aware that she is ill. It is her maids who call the doctor. When Lady Macbeth dies, she is off stage, suggesting that she isn't important to Macbeth any more. Their relationship goes from being close and passionate, to falling apart, like everything else in their world.

AO1 A good, if somewhat rushed, conclusion

MID LEVEL

Comment:
A clear answer which shows knowledge of the text with some basic interpretation of the extract and the play as a whole. Quotations are generally embedded, although there is one unnecessarily long quotation. Several points explain effects or make relevant comments on Shakespeare's use of language in selected quotations. However, very little reference to context is made.

For a Good Level:

■ Comment more frequently on how Shakespeare has used language, form and structure to present this relationship.

■ Analyse the language more closely – look at the particular words Shakespeare uses and consider the reasons why.

■ Try connecting more points about the extract to elsewhere in the play, in order to achieve more depth through comparison.

■ Make more developed use of historical, social and literary contexts.

Sample answer B

The relationship between Macbeth and Lady Macbeth is a complex one that changes as the play progresses. Act I Scene 7 marks the second time we meet the pair together. The scene is at a crucial moment in the play and is one where we see Lady Macbeth dominating the relationship.

> **AO1** Clear opening, focusing on the extract and the question

Although this extract begins with a clear statement of intent from Macbeth – 'We will proceed no further in this business' – he is soon swayed by his wife's arguments. His use of the first person plural 'we' suggests that he expects his wife to play a subservient role and agree with his decision. However, Lady Macbeth has already renounced her femininity in Act I Scene 5 and will not bow down to society's expectations of her gender. She will not obey in the way Macbeth seems to expect her to. In her attack she uses the second person 'you', making it clear that she is not the one who is backing out.

> **AO2** Close analysis of language
>
> **AO3** Relevant link to context
>
> **AO2** Linguistic terminology
>
> **AO1** Relevant reference to elsewhere in play
>
> **AO4** Slightly informal expression

The position Lady Macbeth holds in the relationship is shown through Shakespeare's use of a list of rapid rhetorical questions that charge her speech with power. In just eleven lines, she questions her husband's courage, painting him 'green and pale', colours associated with sickness; challenges his love; and accuses him of cowardice. The fact that she knows exactly where to hurt Macbeth, shows the closeness of their relationship. She plays on his sense of pride, using words like 'valour' and 'dare' that we already know are important parts of Macbeth's reputation and sense of identity.

> **AO2** Confident use of terminology
>
> **AO2** Close attention to effect of phrase
>
> **AO2** Explains effect of language
>
> **AO1** Refers to question

In his response, Macbeth echoes the words that are most important to him: 'I dare do'. He is proud of his ability to act with daring, as described by the Captain previously. He is repeatedly associated with the verb 'to do'. He has shown on the battlefield that 'who dares do more is none'. He was the only one who was fierce enough to kill the enemy. Now that idea of him as a man of action is challenged by his wife. This creates an imbalance which Macbeth seeks to right. At the time when the play is set, women were supposed to be the weaker sex and Macbeth cannot be defeated by his wife.

> **AO1** Neatly refers to other parts of play
>
> **AO2** Close attention to language, though this could be analysed in more detail
>
> **AO3** Reference to context

However, when Lady Macbeth persists with her challenge, it shows that she is at least his equal. Later, he says that she should 'bring forth men-children only!', suggesting that she is so bold that her children would be great warriors.

> **AO1** Refers to later part of scene – this could be linked more closely to the question

Later in the play we see the relationship shift. Whereas Lady Macbeth manipulates Macbeth in this scene and

> **AO1** Traces the development of the relationship, though could be more specific as to the exact points

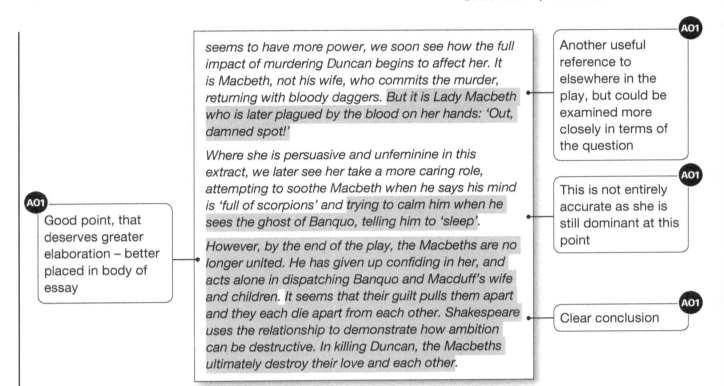

AO1

seems to have more power, we soon see how the full impact of murdering Duncan begins to affect her. It is Macbeth, not his wife, who commits the murder, returning with bloody daggers. But it is Lady Macbeth who is later plagued by the blood on her hands: 'Out, damned spot!'

Another useful reference to elsewhere in the play, but could be examined more closely in terms of the question

Where she is persuasive and unfeminine in this extract, we later see her take a more caring role, attempting to soothe Macbeth when he says his mind is 'full of scorpions' and trying to calm him when he sees the ghost of Banquo, telling him to 'sleep'.

AO1

This is not entirely accurate as she is still dominant at this point

AO1

Good point, that deserves greater elaboration – better placed in body of essay

However, by the end of the play, the Macbeths are no longer united. He has given up confiding in her, and acts alone in dispatching Banquo and Macduff's wife and children. It seems that their guilt pulls them apart and they each die apart from each other. Shakespeare uses the relationship to demonstrate how ambition can be destructive. In killing Duncan, the Macbeths ultimately destroy their love and each other.

AO1

Clear conclusion

GOOD LEVEL

Comment:

This is a well-constructed answer which explores some aspects of the extract in detail and brings in relevant ideas from across the whole play. In places, ideas are well probed and expression is generally good, with quotations used particularly well. There is analysis of Shakespeare's use of language and some appropriate reference to context.

For a High Level:

- Develop ideas more fully and aim for detailed and close analysis.
- Link interpretative points to Shakespeare's use of language, form and structure throughout the answer – remember that AO2 is as important as AO1.
- Try to bring ideas about the social context even more thoroughly into the argument.

Sample answer C

This scene shows a relationship that was unusual for both Shakespeare's time and the medieval era in which 'Macbeth' is set. Whereas women were expected to be subservient, Shakespeare presents a key moment in their relationship when the female partner, Lady Macbeth, is dominant. However, this is not sustained throughout the play, and we get a very different sense of them by the closing scenes.

AO1 — Clear and cogent introduction

AO1 — Focuses on question

Before this extract, in Act I Scene 5, Lady Macbeth invokes the spirits of darkness to 'unsex' her, an unnatural and disturbing act for a contemporary audience. Her role is not one of submissive femininity. In fact, she links Macbeth to the feminine image of 'milk', accusing him of 'kindness' and is herself aligned with the masculine motif of 'blood'. The fact that this is something she cannot ultimately wash away might suggest that fighting gender stereotypes is destructive, rather than constructive, but whatever the interpretation the Macbeths' relationship is askew in many ways.

AO3 — Incorporates reference to context

AO2 — Competent use of literary terminology

AO1 — Sustained response to question

In this extract, we see the relationship's imbalance. Prior to this extract, Shakespeare shows Macbeth expressing his doubts about murdering Duncan in a soliloquy. That solitude contrasts with this next part of the scene which Macbeth shares with his 'dearest partner of greatness', who disregards his doubts. Although Macbeth seems unequivocal that 'We will proceed no further in this business', Lady Macbeth is determined that they will. Macbeth might have 'carved out his passage' on the battlefield, but he cannot 'carve' through the strength of his wife's rhetoric.

AO1 — Embeds quotations from elsewhere in play

AO1 — Shows full awareness of writer and techniques

AO4 — Sophisticated language and phrasing

She hurls questions at him, starting with 'Was the hope drunk / Wherein you dressed yourself?' The repetition of the plosive 'd' emphasises her disdain. Where Macbeth uses the inclusive pronoun 'we', Lady Macbeth uses the accusatory second person, 'you'. Only at the end of the scene, when she has won Macbeth over, does she shift into the plural 'we', showing that they are again two halves of one whole.

AO2 — Linguistic terminology

AO2 — Analyses effects of language

AO2 — Close analysis of language

Lady Macbeth also uses her husband's reputation to taunt him with the negative 'I dare not' and the modal verb 'I would', words that seem weak and unmanly in a warrior culture. Macbeth seems to pray to his wife to stop, 'Prithee peace', suggesting that she has a godlike power over him. It seems he is prepared to sacrifice everything for her opinion of him, stating, 'I dare do all that may become a man.' In this way, Shakespeare uses the relationship to create a complexity in the audience's response to the tragic hero: Macbeth is not entirely evil, nor driven by ambition; he is also driven by love – or at the very least his status in the relationship.

AO1 — Understanding of character

AO3 — Links to context

AO2 — Linguistic terminology

AO1 — Thoughtful response that examines writer's intentions

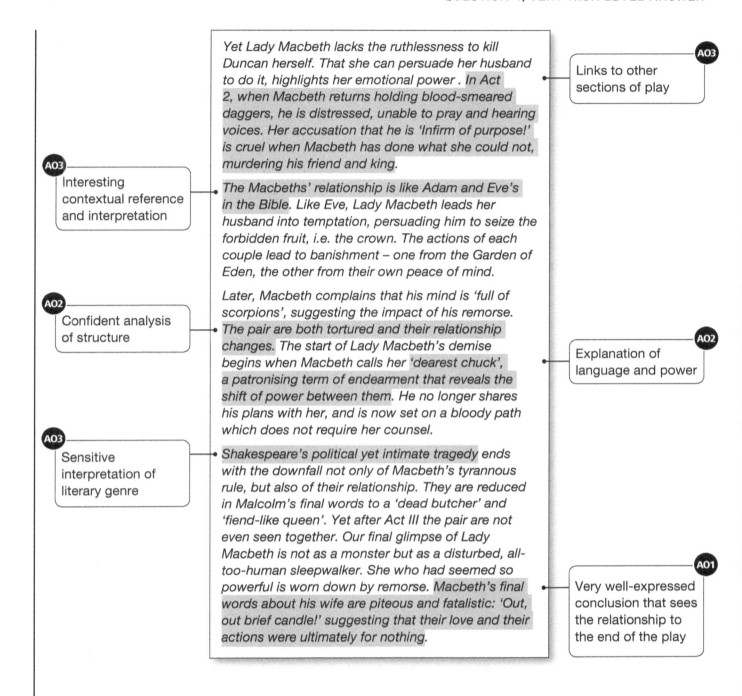

AO3 — Interesting contextual reference and interpretation

AO2 — Confident analysis of structure

AO3 — Sensitive interpretation of literary genre

AO3 — Links to other sections of play

AO2 — Explanation of language and power

AO1 — Very well-expressed conclusion that sees the relationship to the end of the play

Yet Lady Macbeth lacks the ruthlessness to kill Duncan herself. That she can persuade her husband to do it, highlights her emotional power . In Act 2, when Macbeth returns holding blood-smeared daggers, he is distressed, unable to pray and hearing voices. Her accusation that he is 'Infirm of purpose!' is cruel when Macbeth has done what she could not, murdering his friend and king.

The Macbeths' relationship is like Adam and Eve's in the Bible. Like Eve, Lady Macbeth leads her husband into temptation, persuading him to seize the forbidden fruit, i.e. the crown. The actions of each couple lead to banishment – one from the Garden of Eden, the other from their own peace of mind.

Later, Macbeth complains that his mind is 'full of scorpions', suggesting the impact of his remorse. The pair are both tortured and their relationship changes. The start of Lady Macbeth's demise begins when Macbeth calls her 'dearest chuck', a patronising term of endearment that reveals the shift of power between them. He no longer shares his plans with her, and is now set on a bloody path which does not require her counsel.

Shakespeare's political yet intimate tragedy ends with the downfall not only of Macbeth's tyrannous rule, but also of their relationship. They are reduced in Malcolm's final words to a 'dead butcher' and 'fiend-like queen'. Yet after Act III the pair are not even seen together. Our final glimpse of Lady Macbeth is not as a monster but as a disturbed, all-too-human sleepwalker. She who had seemed so powerful is worn down by remorse. Macbeth's final words about his wife are piteous and fatalistic: 'Out, out brief candle!' suggesting that their love and their actions were ultimately for nothing.

VERY HIGH LEVEL

Comment:
This is a highly convincing answer which shows clear understanding of the whole text and draws confidently from it throughout. Quotations are embedded, well selected and analysed, and there is thoughtful and sometimes original interpretation of ideas and issues. Contexts are used appropriately and fluently woven in.

PART THREE: FURTHER YORK NOTES PRACTICE TESTS WITH SHORT ANSWERS

Here are three further questions on the text in a similar style to the ones you might face in your exam. Taking into account what you have learned from the mark schemes on pages 7–8, and the sample responses to the other questions, use Questions 5 to 7 as you wish. You may choose to:

- plan ideas
- write opening paragraphs or part answers
- write full answers at your own speed
- write full answers to a set time limit.

Once you have finished, you can check to see if you have covered some of the key points suggested in the Answers section, and make a judgement about what level you have achieved.

Question 5

Read the following extract from Act I Scene 5 of *Macbeth* and then answer the question that follows.

At this point in the play, Lady Macbeth has just received a letter from her husband, describing his meeting with the witches on the heath.

LADY MACBETH

Glamis thou art, and Cawdor, and shalt be

What thou art promised. Yet do I fear thy nature:

It is too full o'the milk of human-kindness

To catch the nearest way. Thou wouldst be great,

5   Art not without ambition, but without

The illness should attend it. What thou wouldst highly

That wouldst thou holily, wouldst not play false,

And yet wouldst wrongly win. Thou'dst have, great
    Glamis,

That which cries, 'Thus thou must do' if thou have it,

10   And that which rather thou dost fear to do

Than wishest should be undone. Hie thee hither

That I may pour my spirits in thine ear,

And chastise with the valour of my tongue

All that impedes thee from the golden round

15   Which fate and metaphysical aid doth seem

To have thee crowned withal.

Starting with this speech, explain how far you think Shakespeare presents Lady Macbeth as ruthless.

Write about:

- how far Shakespeare presents Lady Macbeth as ruthless in this speech
- how far Shakespeare presents Lady Macbeth as ruthless in the play as a whole.

[30 marks]
AO4 [4 marks]

Question 6

Read the following extract from Act IV Scene 1 of *Macbeth* and then answer the question that follows.

At this point in the play, Macbeth is visiting the witches and asking for further prophecies.

THIRD APPARITION

Macbeth shall never vanquished be, until

Great Birnam Wood to high Dunsinane Hill

Shall come against him.   *He descends*

MACBETH

                              That will never be.

Who can impress the forest, bid the tree

5   Unfix his earth-bound root? Sweet bodements! Good!

Rebellious dead rise never till the wood

Of Birnam rise, and our high-placed Macbeth

Shall live the lease of nature, pay his breath

To time and mortal custom. Yet my heart

10   Throbs to know one thing: tell me, if your art

Can tell so much, shall Banquo's issue ever

Reign in this kingdom?

ALL

                              Seek to know no more.

MACBETH

I will be satisfied! Deny me this

And an eternal curse fall on you!

Starting with this moment in the play, explain how far you think Shakespeare presents fate as responsible for Macbeth's downfall.

Write about:

- how Shakespeare presents fate in this extract
- how Shakespeare presents fate in the play as a whole.

[30 marks]
AO4 [4 marks]

Question 7

Read the following extract from Act IV Scene 3 of *Macbeth* and then answer the question that follows.

At this point in the play, Macduff has fled to England and Malcolm. They are talking about the need for a new leader of Scotland.

> **MALCOLM**
>
>   But I have none.
> The king-becoming graces,
> As justice, verity, temperance, stableness,
> Bounty, perseverance, mercy, lowliness,
> 5 Devotion, patience, courage, fortitude,
> I have no relish of them, but abound
> In the division of each several crime,
> Acting it many ways. Nay, had I power, I should
> Pour the sweet milk of concord into hell,
> 10 Uproar the universal peace, confound
> All unity on earth.
>
> **MACDUFF**
>
>   O Scotland, Scotland!
>
> **MALCOLM**
>
> If such a one be fit to govern, speak.
> I am as I have spoken.
>
> **MACDUFF**
>
>   Fit to govern!
> No, not to live. O nation miserable,
> 15 With an untitled tyrant, bloody-sceptred,
> When shalt thou see thy wholesome days again,
> Since that the truest issue of thy throne
> By his own interdiction stands accused
> And does blaspheme his breed? Thy royal father
> 20 Was a most sainted king; the queen that bore thee,
> Oftener upon her knees than on her feet,
> Died every day she lived. Fare thee well!
> These evils thou repeat'st upon thyself
> Have banished me from Scotland. O my breast,
> 25 Thy hope ends here!

Starting with this conversation, write about how Shakespeare presents ideas about leadership.

Write about:

- how Shakespeare presents ideas about leadership in this extract
- how Shakespeare presents ideas about leadership in the play as a whole.

[30 marks]
AO4 [4 marks]

ANSWERS

Short (indicative content) answers are given for Questions 5 to 7 below, covering the three main Assessment Objectives.

Question 5

Your answer could include the following:

AO1

■ In the extract, Lady Macbeth's excitement about Macbeth's news shows her willingness to 'catch the nearest way' to power.

■ Lady Macbeth is instrumental in the death of Duncan – in this extract, she seizes on the idea of accelerating fate.

■ Lady Macbeth's ambition is to see her husband crowned king – and her own ambition is to be his 'partner of greatness'.

■ Lady Macbeth wields considerable power over her husband, seen for example in 'pour my spirits in thine ear' and 'chastise thee'. This power changes in the course of the play, just as their relationship changes.

■ There is a powerful contrast between Lady Macbeth's ruthlessness here and later in the play when she is plagued by guilt, culminating in her sleepwalking in Act V Scene1 and subsequent taking of her own life.

AO2

■ The use of soliloquy to present Lady Macbeth allows her inner thoughts to be shown – in comparison to the way Macbeth is introduced by others before he appears.

■ Lady Macbeth's language echoes the way the witches greet Macbeth in Act I Scene 3, so aligning her with the witches from the first time we meet her.

■ Her metaphor describing Macbeth as 'full o'the milk of human-kindness' establishes the contrast between Macbeth's nature and her own ruthless nature at this point.

■ The repetition of modal verb tenses such as 'wouldst' suggests that in Macbeth's hands the future is uncertain and contrasts with Lady Macbeth's 'Thou must do it', which again suggests her power to command her husband.

AO3

■ Social expectations of women at the time included being submissive, particularly with regard to their husband; Lady Macbeth has many masculine attributes – ruthlessness was not considered feminine.

■ A Jacobean audience would expect a wife to fulfil a maternal, loving role. However, Lady Macbeth is powerful and murderous.

■ Ambition is another trait Jacobean audiences would have considered masculine, yet it is Lady Macbeth who appears more ambitious in this scene (compare with Macbeth in Act I Scene 7).

■ In breaching these gender stereotypes, is it Lady Macbeth who is ultimately responsible for the death of Duncan?

Question 6

Your answer could include the following:

AO1

- Macbeth has sought out the witches and demanded to be shown the future. Is it his own free will that brought him there, or was he destined to return to them?

- The apparitions offer three new prophecies – but it is in Macbeth's hands to interpret and act on them. Their earlier predictions had suggested that Macbeth would become king but Macbeth and his wife take things into their own hands by killing Duncan.

- Macbeth is paranoid about Banquo's children and it is his belief in fate that leads him to send murderers to kill Banquo and Fleance.

- Macbeth's own brutality as a leader leads to his downfall – it is free will that leads him to murder Macduff's family, not fate.

- Macbeth fails to recognise that fate is inevitable. He tries to manipulate the future, but is unable to. Would he have become king as the witches prophesised, without murdering Duncan?

AO2

- Shakespeare makes the language of the prophecies confusing, so they are like riddles, leaving it open to interpretation whether they are accurate prophecies or whether Macbeth is taking matters into his own hands.

- The stage direction *'He descends'* after each apparition emphasises the influence each one will have over Macbeth.

- Macbeth's exclamations show his confidence in the predictions – 'Sweet bodements! Good!' – implying that he embraces fate.

- Macbeth's curse at the end of the extract shows his narcissistic sense of power and control – he thinks he can control fate itself.

- The use of iambic pentameter suggests Macbeth's sense of conviction at this point.

- The pattern of three prophecies echoes the opening scenes of the play.

AO3

- Society's belief in supernatural forces at the time is reflected in the ways that fate appears to rule Macbeth.

- It is Macbeth's fatal flaw as hero in this tragedy.

- Shakespeare's investigation of the roles of determinism and free will, i.e. the debate as to whether one is responsible for one's own actions or subject to the whims of fate and fortune, is central to the play.

Question 7

Your answer could include the following:

AO1

- Malcolm lists the desired characteristics of a good leader.
- Malcolm tests Macduff's loyalty by saying he himself would be a bad leader.
- The presentation of Duncan as a good leader refers back to Macbeth's soliloquy in Act I Scene 7.
- Shakespeare uses the contrast between Duncan and Macbeth to present good leadership in the play as a whole and to emphasise the tyranny of Macbeth.

AO2

- Shakespeare uses abstract nouns to show the qualities of leadership – like a litany.
- The 'milk' imagery echoes Lady Macbeth's description of her husband's nature in Act I Scene 5.
- Macduff's exclamation – 'O Scotland, Scotland!' – shows his loyalty and his despair at what has happened to his country under Macbeth's tyrannous rule.
- It is ironic that Malcolm is listing leadership qualities that in fact he does have himself.

AO3

- The qualities of good leadership are one of the key themes of the play.
- The theme was particularly relevant at the time, with the accession of James VI of Scotland to the throne of England, creating the kingdom of Great Britain.
- Society's attitudes to leadership can appear conflicting – compare the role of warrior kings in medieval Britain with the kindly, generous king Shakespeare presents in Duncan.